RZIM Critical Questions Discussion Guides

Can I Trust the Bible?

Darrell L. Bock

SERIES EDITOR Ravi Zacharias

GENERAL EDITOR Danielle DuRant

Inter-Varsity Press
Nottingham, England

An imprint of InterVarsity Press
Downers Grove, Illinois

InterVarsity Press
P.O. Box 1400, Downers Grove, IL 60515-1426
World Wide Web: www.ivpress.com
Email: email@ivpress.com

Inter-Varsity Press, England
Norton Street, Nottingham NG7 3HR, England
Website: www.ivpbooks.com
Email: ivp@ivpbooks.com

Published in association with the literary agency of Wolgemuth & Associates, Inc., Orlando, Florida.

InterVarsity Press® is the book-publishing division of InterVarsity Christian Fellowship/USA®, a student movement active on campus at hundreds of universities, colleges and schools of nursing in the United States of America, and a member movement of the International Fellowship of Evangelical Students. For information about local and regional activities, write Public Relations Dept., InterVarsity Christian Fellowship/USA, 6400 Schroeder Rd., P.O. Box 7895, Madison, WI 53707-7895, or visit the IVCF website at <www.intervarsity.org>.

Inter-Varsity Press, England, is closely linked with the Universities and Colleges Christian Fellowship, a student movement connecting Christian Unions in universities and colleges throughout Great Britain, and a member movement of the International Fellowship of Evangelical Students. Website: www.uccf.org.uk.

Adapted from Darrell Bock, Can I Trust the Bible? *(Norcross, Ga.: RZIM, 2001).*

Design: Cindy Kiple
Images: David Buffington/Getty Images

USA ISBN 978-0-8308-3152-4
UK ISBN 978-1-84474-221-9

Printed in the United States of America ∞

P 19 18 17 16 15 14 13 12 11 10 9 8 7 6 5 4 3 2
Y 23 22 21 20 19 18 17 16 15 14 13 12 11 10 09 08 07

Contents

Introduction

I was at an airport looking for my departure gate, and I noticed that the flight listed was to another city. So I asked a passenger if that flight was headed to Atlanta or elsewhere. She promptly answered my question and told me the notation was wrong. As I thanked her and turned to find a seat, she said, "Are you Ravi Zacharias?" I answered yes. Then came this utterly surprising response: "I listen to you on the radio regularly. I didn't know you had questions as well." I laughed at her compliment and assured her that I had several questions, especially if I want to get to the right destination.

There are so many answers out there and a question to every answer. To ask them is to engage with information. To ask questions about life's ultimate questions is to be in the pursuit of God. That's what this series is about: to take you to the heart and mind of God, which is the right destination.

In this series, critical questions raised by thinking minds are answered by those who have asked them themselves, and found the answer in the person and teaching of Jesus Christ. There are writers in this series that I have heavily leaned on myself. They are trained in the art of critical thinking not merely for the intellectual stimulation it brings but for the ultimate pursuit: the bridge between the heart and the mind so that thinking shapes being, which in turn impels doing.

In our time such helps as this series are invaluable. On every side, be it the academy or the movies, just enough doubt is cast on the person of Jesus that minds are left unsteadied in their trust in the Scriptures and the truth claims of the gospel. Such doubts and questionings are rarely answered by a one-blow argument. Life is not as simple as that. In fact, any worldview that depends on one such knockout argument flirts with logical and experiential extinction.

Life closes in on us from multiple sides. That is why a good apologetic starts with the fundamentals before it deals with the specifics. From the nature of truth to the incarnation of it in Jesus, from the trustworthiness of the Scriptures to the questions of moral reasoning, they are addressed here. These succinct and interactive discussion guides will stir your mind and occupy a much-used section in your library.

I sincerely hope this series will be both a tool of equipment and a source of inspiration. Darrell Bock in his study *Can I Trust the Bible?* sums up the content of these slender volumes well:

> If there is the possibility that God has spoken through this text and has participated in the history it records, then the answers to our questions are not a mere academic exercise. Our journey back into these seemingly foreign, ancient times may be a real opportunity to see more clearly who we are and were created to be.

A couple words of appreciation are well in order. First, the original effort in putting this all together was done by Paul Copan. In this instance, the hard work as general editor is by Danielle DuRant, who labored long to make this accessible. I am also grateful to InterVarsity Press for seeing the value in this short series and taking the step to publish it. Those of us who study this material will be the beneficiaries.

Questions will haunt as long as the mind is alive. The answers of Christ will inspire and instruct because he is the author of life.

Ravi Zacharias

Getting the Most Out of This Guide

In his booklet *Can I Trust the Bible?* (Norcross, Ga.: RZIM, 2001), Darrell Bock insightfully suggests, "If there is the possibility that God has spoken through this text and has participated in the history it records, then the answers to our question are not a mere academic exercise. Our journey back into these seemingly foreign, ancient times may be a real opportunity to see more clearly who we are and were created to be." The Scriptures reveal to us such a view of knowledge as well: our knowledge of God, our world and ourselves is relational and very human. We are persons in relation to other persons, and we know subjects in relation to other subjects. We do not merely know propositions "out there"—for example, "the water is cold," "God exists"—for to assert such statements necessarily implies some sort of relationship with their subjects.

This discussion guide proposes that "the Bible is trustworthy." We will thus look at the internal and external evidence for its historicity and authenticity, along with Jesus' own words on the matter. As knowing implies understanding, we will consider the message we encounter in each of the passages in order to act on what we have discovered. Or, as Bock suggests, "to see more clearly who we are and were created to be."

SUGGESTIONS FOR INDIVIDUAL STUDY

1. As you begin each session, pray that God will speak to you through his Word.
2. Read the introduction to the session and respond to the opening reflection question or exercise. This is designed to help you focus on God and on the theme of the session.
3. Each session considers a particular passage or passages of Scripture, and is supplemented by the author's commentary. Read and reread the text before engaging the questions.
4. Write your answers to the questions in the spaces provided or in a personal journal. Writing can bring clarity and deeper understanding of yourself and of God's Word.
5. It might be good to have a Bible dictionary handy. Use it to look up any unfamiliar words, names or places.

SUGGESTIONS FOR MEMBERS OF A GROUP STUDY

1. Come to the study prepared. Follow the suggestions for individual study mentioned above. You will find that careful preparation will greatly enrich your time spent in group discussion.
2. Be willing to participate in the discussion. The leader of your group will not be lecturing. Instead, he or she will be encouraging the members of the group to discuss what they have learned. The leader will be asking the questions that are found in this guide.
3. Stick to the topic being discussed. Your answers should be based on the texts provided and not on outside authorities such as

commentaries or speakers. Only rarely should you refer to other portions of the Bible. This allows for everyone to participate in in-depth study on equal ground.

4. Be sensitive to the other members of the group. Listen attentively when they describe what they have learned. You may be surprised by their insights! Each question assumes a variety of answers. Many questions do not have "right" answers, particularly questions that aim at meaning or application. Instead the questions push us to explore the topic more thoroughly. When possible, link what you say to the comments of others. Also, be affirming whenever you can. This will encourage some of the more hesitant members of the group to participate.

5. Be careful not to dominate the discussion. We are sometimes so eager to express our thoughts that we leave too little opportunity for others to respond. By all means participate! But allow others to also.

6. Expect God to teach you through the material being discussed and through the other members of the group. Pray that you will have an enjoyable and profitable time together, but also that as a result of the study you will find ways that you can take action individually and/or as a group.

7. Remember that anything said in the group is considered confidential and should not be discussed outside the group unless specific permission is given to do so.

8. If you are the group leader, you will find additional suggestions at the back of the guide.

1 How Did We Get the Bible We Have?

MATTHEW 5:17-20

Reading a book from the past is like taking a journey to another land. For all its timelessness, the Bible also has that distant feel to it. After all, it was written over two millennia ago. Its roots do go back to a different time and place.

All of that distance raises questions about whether or not what I read really belongs only to such a distant world. Does the Bible really reflect what that world was like, much less what my world is like? So it is natural to ask the question if the Bible is really trustworthy in its content.

■ OPEN

What book took you on your favorite journey as a child? Where did you go?

■ STUDY

Nearly two thousand years ago, the apostle Matthew listened to Jesus on the Sermon on the Mount and recorded his words, which we find in chapters 5-7 of Matthew's Gospel. Jesus' teaching is sometimes perplexing: "Blessed are the poor in spirit." "Blessed are those who mourn." "Blessed are the meek." He calls his disciples "the salt of the earth" and "the light of the world."

Then Jesus says this: "Do not think that I am doing away with what the Law or Prophets taught, for I am the fulfillment of all their teaching." ***Read Matthew 5:17-20.***

[17]"Do not think that I have come to abolish the Law or the Prophets; I have not come to abolish them but to fulfill them. [18]I tell you the truth, until heaven and earth disappear, not the smallest letter, not the least stroke of a pen, will by any means disappear from the Law until everything is accomplished. [19]Anyone who breaks one of the least of these commandments and teaches others to do the same will be called least in the kingdom of heaven, but whoever practices and teaches these commands will be called great in the kingdom of heaven. [20]For I tell you that unless your righteousness surpasses that of the Pharisees and the teachers of the law, you will certainly not enter the kingdom of heaven."

1. What does Jesus mean when he speaks of "the Law and the Prophets"?

2. How does Jesus see his teaching and ministry in relation to the Scriptures?

3. If you had been with the group listening to Jesus, what do you think your response would have been after he spoke these words in verse 17? Confusion? Doubt? Fear?

The term *canon* means a "measuring reed" and refers to a standard that is applied to some topic. When biblical books are described as the canon, they are identified as those books that the church has for centuries looked to as revealing God's way and will, those works inspired by God. The books contained in the Bible were written over a period of about fifteen hundred years, up through the first century A.D. The New Testament canon contains twenty-seven books. Once it was finalized in the mid-fourth century, it has never been challenged—until recently.

When it comes to what we call the Old Testament, the process of recognition of sacred books was pretty much complete by the time of Christ.

4. How were the biblical books of the canon recognized?

5. Note again the statement, "When it comes to what we call the Old Testament, the process of recognition of sacred books was pretty much complete by the time of Christ." What does this information tell us about Jesus' audience and their knowledge of the Scriptures?

6. Read again Matthew 5:17-18. What does this passage reveal about Jesus' own view of the reliability and authority of the Scriptures?

The initial message of the first Christians combined a message about what Jesus said and did with what was written in "the Scripture." In effect, the earliest Christians accepted the sacred books of Judaism as their Scripture. The books we now possess were consistently named as Scripture, with only a few books being disputed now and then as to whether they should be included. The rule seems to have been, *If a book is really in doubt, leave it out.*

The canon emerged through a long and careful process of reflection in which the church, considering what it believed and what these books taught, embraced some as reflective of its faith in a way that caused it to recognize, receive and affirm their inspiration. By the end of the second century, the core of what became the New Testament was recognized. Many other works continued to be assessed in the next two centuries that followed. The list of recognized books, once it emerged, has since served as the New Testament.

7. Does the idea that "the rule seems to have been—*if a book is really in doubt, leave it out*" give you more or less confidence in the reliability of the Scriptures? Why?

8. Have you ever wondered whether the Bible is really God's Word—his personal revelation to you? When does this question seem to surface for you?

9. Read again Matthew 5:19. The NIV says, "Anyone who *breaks* one of the least of these commandments"; other Bible translations read "relaxes" or "annuls." With these additional word pictures, summarize what you think Jesus is saying in this passage.

10. What is the connection between "practices" and "teaches" in verse 19 with "righteousness" in verse 20?

11. Jesus says in Matthew 5:6, "Blessed are those who hunger and thirst for righteousness, for they will be filled." In what ways is righteousness a good thing? Why does Jesus want people to be righteous?

12. Look again at your response to question 3. After studying this passage, has your response to Jesus' words changed or remained the same? Explain.

GOING FURTHER

Journal or consider some of the questions you have about God and the Bible, perhaps giving more attention to the second part of question 8: *When* does this question seem to surface for you?

Additional Reading

Michael Green, *The Books the Church Suppressed* (Grand Rapids: Monarch, 2006).

2 What Are Our Sources?

LUKE 1:1-4; 3:1-6

The Bible is a book both like other books and unlike them. Within its pages there is the acknowledgment that sources of various types stand behind its material. This makes the Bible sound like any book. Luke's admission of sources (Luke 1:1-4) and the fact that he sought to check them is an indication that the writers tried to exercise care in how they presented the text.

■ OPEN

Do you remember playing the "telephone game" as a child in school? (One child whispers a phrase to another and then that child whispers it to the next until the last child in the classroom hears the phrase.) What happened to the phrase from the first to the last whisper?

■ STUDY

Luke informs his readers from the outset how and why he wrote his Gospel. Though he was probably not an eyewitness to Jesus, he sought out others who had been with Jesus in order to produce an accurate record of his life and ministry. From Luke's detailed descriptions of past people and events, historians have been able to verify many of his Gospel's sources and claims. ***Read Luke 1:1-4.***

[1]Many have undertaken to draw up an account of the things that have been fulfilled among us, [2]just as they were handed down to us by those who from the first were eyewitnesses and servants of the word. [3]Therefore, since I myself have carefully investigated everything from the beginning, it seemed good also to me to write an orderly account for you, most excellent Theophilus, [4]so that you may know the certainty of the things you have been taught.

1. What about Luke 1:1-4 suggests that the biblical writers "tried to exercise care in how they presented the text"?

2. What reason does Luke give for writing his Gospel? Note the words Luke uses to describe this undertaking. Is his investigation measured and precise, or casual and spontaneous?

3. If you were "most excellent Theophilus" (or perhaps a friend of his), what might your initial response be upon reading Luke's openings words to you?

In the case of the texts surrounding Jesus, the role of eyewitnesses being at the root of the tradition is strong. Luke himself speaks about how those who began to circulate the stories about Jesus were eyewitnesses and ministers of the Word (Luke 1:2). As we noted, he claimed to be careful about how his work was done. Many writers of the Bible, especially in the New Testament, were people at the events described or people who had access to others who were there. For Mark's Gospel, tradition long held that what is present are the memoirs of Peter's preaching. Matthew has roots in the work of the apostle by that name. John has similar apostolic roots. Remember that, for the New Testament, an apostolic association is important for establishing the account's inclusion in the canon. This standard was because of a concern about the account's credibility.

4. What do you think qualified Luke to write one of the Gospels?

What about Luke's approach made the early church trust his work as credible?

5. What does Luke mean by describing Jesus' eyewitnesses as "servants of the word"? What does this phrase suggest about the Scriptures ("the word")?

Read Luke 3:1-6.

[1]In the fifteenth year of the reign of Tiberius Caesar—when Pontius Pilate was governor of Judea, Herod tetrarch of Galilee, his brother Philip tetrarch of Iturea and Traconitis, and Lysanias tetrarch of Abilene— [2]during the high priesthood of Annas and Caiaphas, the word of God came to John son of Zechariah in the desert. [3]He went into all the country around the Jordan, preaching a baptism of repentance for the forgiveness of sins. [4]As is written in the book of the words of Isaiah the prophet:

"A voice of one calling in the desert,
'Prepare the way for the Lord,
make straight paths for him.
[5]Every valley shall be filled in,
every mountain and hill made low.
The crooked roads shall become straight,
the rough ways smooth.
[6]And all mankind will see God's salvation.'"

6. Before making the point that "the word of God came to John son of Zechariah in the desert," Luke offers a lengthy introduction. Why do you think he includes so many names and details?

7. Luke (along with fellow Gospel writers Matthew and Mark) records the life of John the Baptist. According to verse 3, what is his ministry?

8. What does Luke's inclusion of a source from Isaiah (see verses 4-6) tell us about John as well as Jesus?

This connection to actual witnesses is not the case with all the books of the Bible, perhaps even much of it. Some of its contents were passed on by oral tradition or through sources.

That such passing on of a text or an account could be exact is indicated in the history of the Old Testament text. For years our oldest manuscripts of the Old Testament came from the tenth century A.D. (known as the Masoretic Text). Claims were made that the text was in a terrific degree of oral flux with things added to or subtracted from the text on a regular basis. When the Dead Sea Scrolls were discovered in the 1940s, such theories could be tested with actual documents that leapt over a thousand years of transmission history, as the documents found in these caves were that much older than what we had previously. The copies of Isaiah found at the caves of Qumran were virtual matches for their thousand-year younger descendants. The text tradition for the Hebrew text had remained stable for a millennium.

9. How did the discovery of the Isaiah manuscripts at Qumran confirm the trustworthiness of biblical oral and written sources?

10. As we have observed—and as Luke himself tells us—the biblical authors occasionally relied on one another as sources about historical events and Jesus and his ministry. Recall the telephone game: if you needed to pass along life-changing information, how might you try to insure accuracy in its communcation?

11. Imagine again that you are Theophilus, whom Luke writes to "so that you may know the certainty of the things you have been taught." How might this study change your understanding or confidence of the Scriptures?

■ GOING FURTHER

Read Luke 1—3 slowly and note (or even underline) the numerous specific historic details that Luke provides to introduce his readers to Jesus and his ministry.

Additional Reading

Amy Orr-Ewing, *Is the Bible Intolerant?* (Downers Grove, Ill.: InterVarsity Press, 2006). See especially chapters three and four on the reliability of biblical manuscripts.

3 What Do We Mean by *Inspiration?*

2 PETER 1:16-21

The concept of inspiration entails a claim that God has involved himself in the process of producing Scripture. God speaks through the human writers.

■ OPEN

What's your working definition of *inspiration?* Have you ever experienced a "moment of inspiration" or known someone who has? Describe this experience and why you might have considered it "inspiration."

■ STUDY

Simon Peter left his fishing nets to follow Jesus and was an eyewitness to the cross and many miracles. He pens his second letter to remind the church of their calling and to warn them of false prophets "denying the sovereign Lord who bought them" (2:1). Declaring the preeminence of the written word, Peter writes down what he has witnessed so that after his death his readers "will always be able to remember these things" (1:15). ***Read 2 Peter 1:16-21.***

[16]*We did not follow cleverly invented stories when we told you about*

the power and coming of our Lord Jesus Christ, but we were eyewitnesses of his majesty. [17]For he received honor and glory from God the Father when the voice came to him from the Majestic Glory, saying, "This is my Son, whom I love; with him I am well pleased." [18]We ourselves heard this voice that came from heaven when we were with him on the sacred mountain.

[19]And we have the word of the prophets made more certain, and you will do well to pay attention to it, as to a light shining in a dark place, until the day dawns and the morning star rises in your hearts. [20]Above all, you must understand that no prophecy of Scripture came about by the prophet's own interpretation. [21]For prophecy never had its origin in the will of man, but men spoke from God as they were carried along by the Holy Spirit.

1. How did Peter obtain his knowledge of Jesus and his ministry?

2. What event does Peter allude to in verses 16 to 18?

3. Notice the particular words and phrases that the apostle uses to describe his time with Jesus. How would you characterize his tone and response to what he has witnessed?

The concept of inspiration entails a claim that God has involved himself in the process of producing Scripture. God speaks through the human writers. However, the Bible also discusses how this claim for a divine role works. The divine superintention of the Bible's content does not mean that God is dictating the words of Scripture, but that he has motivated its content down to the wording of its message (2 Timothy 3:16-17). Second Peter 1:20-21 speaks of men being borne along by the Spirit who spoke from God. Like the wind drives a boat through its sail, God gives the Scripture its initiative, path and direction; but there still is a human author who mans the helm. Anyone reading the Bible can see the variety of styles that mark its pages. To argue that the Bible is a book inspired by God does not dismiss the human elements that make up the book. Still, it is one thing to make claims, yet another to see if there are reasons to suggest that those claims should be embraced.

4. How does your working definition of *inspiration* fit alongside the above description of the process? How does it compare to Peter's understanding of inspiration?

5. Explain the sailing metaphor that Peter uses to portray the process of biblical inspiration. What other images or metaphors help you to visualize this process?

6. The apostle writes in verse 19, "And we have the word of the prophets made more certain." What does he mean by this assertion? Notice the comparison he makes regarding what brings a greater degree of certainty (see verses 17-18). Does his assertion surprise you?

As cultural fads ebb and flow, the inescapable truth emerges that century after century the power of the written Word has surpassed, and will continue to surpass, the exhilarations of momentary experience, which are conceived and die in an instant. We tenderly set a halo on the forehead of feeling or miracle, but in times of greatest loss it is the written Word that carries us through, not feeling. The apostle Peter himself in his epistle reminds us of this very truth. We must remember that this is the same Peter who experienced the ecstasy of the transfiguration—a sight that caused him to plead that he and those with him be permitted to permanently bask in its afterglow. It is Peter who, contrasting the temporariness of that experience with the eternal and unfading brilliance of the Word, says, "We now have the more sure word of prophecy." Inscripturation has a present and eternal point of reference, transcending mere flashes of feeling or of the miraculous.[1]

7. "Inscripturation" is the period of time in which the Scriptures came into being, from the moment of inspiration to the penning of words to parchment. How does having inspired truth

[1]Ravi Zacharias, "Biblical Authority and Our Cultural Crisis," *Just Thinking*, fall 1993 (available online at <www.rzim.org/publications/jttran.php?seqid=14>).

anchored in a document answer the problem of "exhilarations of momentary experience, which are conceived and die in an instant"?

8. Look again at verses 16 and 20-21. What two forms of expression does Peter reject as being inspired? Why do you think he cites these examples?

9. The Scriptures affirm the certainty and authority of "the word of the prophets" above any experience of God. Do you think that the biblical writers were uniquely inspired? Why or why not?

10. Based on your understanding of the biblical sense of inspiration, how might you evaluate a person or book claiming to be inspired by God?

■ GOING FURTHER

Read the first chapter of 2 Peter and consider how the section studied (verses 16-21) gives weight to the apostle's words earlier in the chapter. What one insight might you journal about or study further?

Additional Reading

Norman Geisler, "Tough Questions About the Bible," in *Who Made God? And Answers to Over 100 Tough Questions of Faith,* ed. Ravi Zacharias and Norman Geisler (Grand Rapids: Zondervan, 2003).

4 What Is the History Behind the Bible?

MATTHEW 21:18-22; MARK 11:12-25

The international conflict that emerged in the second decade of the twentieth century was initially called "The Great War" or the "War to End All Wars." Both names expressed the scope of the conflict, which was unprecedented up to that time. The name this conflict is known by today is "The First World War," a name it could not have until the Second World War took place. Now whether one refers to this event by its original name, The Great War, or by its alternative, The Second World War, one is looking at the same set of historical events.

In history, events have some element of dynamic flow, for their impact and meaning often become clear not from the event itself, but from the subsequent impact of the event. Thus in writing history, one can write from a perspective that is like the way the event was experienced or from a perspective that is aware of its subsequent impact. Each approach is historical but takes on the story with a narrower or larger frame of reference in mind. As such, differing perspectives and details can emerge as each perspective influences which details are picked up.

■ OPEN

Think about a time you've listened to your spouse, family member or good friend retell a particular event you've both experienced. What surprised you about the details that were included or left out?

■ STUDY

Both Matthew and Mark record the cursing of the fig tree in their account of Jesus' last week on earth. Though their retelling of this event is nearly identical, Mark places the incident before Jesus' cleansing of the temple whereas Matthew positions it after. A careful reader will want to consider this distinction while also bearing in mind each writer's unique perspective of Jesus and the themes of their entire Gospels. ***Read Matthew 21:18-22; Mark 11:12-25.***

Matthew 21:18*Early in the morning, as [Jesus] was on his way back to the city, he was hungry.* 19*Seeing a fig tree by the road, he went up to it but found nothing on it except leaves. Then he said to it, "May you never bear fruit again!" Immediately the tree withered.*

20*When the disciples saw this, they were amazed. "How did the fig tree wither so quickly?" they asked.*

21*Jesus replied, "I tell you the truth, if you have faith and do not doubt, not only can you do what was done to the fig tree, but also you can say to this mountain, 'Go, throw yourself into the sea,' and it will be done.* 22*If you believe, you will receive whatever you ask for in prayer."*

Mark 11:12*The next day as they were leaving Bethany, Jesus was hungry.* 13*Seeing in the distance a fig tree in leaf, he went to find out if it had any fruit. When he reached it, he found nothing but leaves, because it was not the season for figs.* 14*Then he said to the tree, "May no one ever eat fruit from you again." And his disciples heard him say it.*

[15]On reaching Jerusalem, Jesus entered the temple area and began driving out those who were buying and selling there. He overturned the tables of the money changers and the benches of those selling doves, [16]and would not allow anyone to carry merchandise through the temple courts. [17]And as he taught them, he said, "Is it not written:

"'My house will be called
a house of prayer for all nations'?

But you have made it 'a den of robbers.'"

[18]The chief priests and the teachers of the law heard this and began looking for a way to kill him, for they feared him, because the whole crowd was amazed at his teaching.

[19]When evening came, they went out of the city.

[20]In the morning, as they went along, they saw the fig tree withered from the roots. [21]Peter remembered and said to Jesus, "Rabbi, look! The fig tree you cursed has withered!"

[22]"Have faith in God," Jesus answered. [23]"I tell you the truth, if anyone says to this mountain, 'Go, throw yourself into the sea,' and does not doubt in his heart but believes that what he says will happen, it will be done for him. [24]Therefore I tell you, whatever you ask for in prayer, believe that you have received it, and it will be yours. [25]And when you stand praying, if you hold anything against anyone, forgive him, so that your Father in heaven may forgive you your sins."

1. Why does Jesus curse the fig tree?

What curious detail about its condition does Mark provide in verse 13?

2. Matthew's Gospel compresses the details of Jesus cursing the fig tree. What does he omit? Why do you think he does this?

3. One of the major themes in Mark's Gospel is the judgment of God and Jesus' unique authority to deliver this judgment (as well as God's salvation). How does Mark's insertion of the incident described in 11:15-18 serve to emphasize this theme?

4. Does it surprise you that the biblical writers recorded historical events with concern not only for accuracy but also for literary effect?

How does this knowledge change your understanding or appreciation of history? Explain.

History, especially when dealing with multiple sources, is not one-dimensional with only one set of possible facts to present. The portrayal of history is framed by what concerns drive the choice of details presented. Many differences between the Gospels, which some reject on the simplistic difference-equals-error formula, are more likely the product of the fact that different writers present different concerns. These distinct concerns lead them to highlight different points of a history that is larger than any one account.

5. Look again at the Gospel passages above. What indications do you see that one Gospel writer is writing "from a perspective that is like the way the event was experienced" and the other "from a perspective that is aware of its subsequent impact"?

Are there tests one can apply to examine an event's or saying's trustworthiness? New Testament scholars often speak of these standards as the "criteria of authenticity." The first standard often noted is the criteria of *multiple attestation.* It looks for events or teaching that is multiply attested, that is, events that have more than one source strand that speak about them.

A second standard is *dissimilarity.* It argues that if a teaching is unlike a person's cultural roots or unlike what came after the person, then it is likely to be authentic. It is the very uniqueness of the teaching that suggests someone else did not create it.

A third standard is *coherence.* Anything that coheres with what the other standards suggest are authentic has good reason to be accepted.

6. Understanding that this is not an exhaustive study, apply each test to the two Gospel passages above. What evidence do you find that Jesus' encounter with the fig tree meets this "criteria of authenticity"?

7. How does this insight change your understanding or appreciation of the relationship of the Holy Spirit and the biblical writers in the process of inspiration?

8. What is one insight from this study that you want to apply or give further thought to this week?

■ GOING FURTHER

Spend some time reading through Mark or another Gospel, tracing the themes the writer develops and particularly the unique way he portrays Jesus. You may want to use a study Bible or commentary to assist you.

Additional Reading

Craig Blomberg, *The Historical Reliability of the Gospels* (Downers Grove, Ill.: InterVarsity Press, 1987).

5 What Does Archaeology Teach Us?

JOHN 5:1-15

Archaeology cannot prove that events took place, but it can show that details noted in events, some of them incidental, fit in the time and culture of the text. It also shows that we should be cautious commenting confidently about errors in the Bible merely because only the Bible attests something. The unearthing of the right site may show that we were working with a very limited pool of knowledge.

■ OPEN

Have you ever visited a historic or picturesque site, such as Yosemite's Redwood Forest or Lake Louise, that you first learned about in the pages of a book? How did it feel to finally experience the place firsthand? What surprised you about the actual place?

■ STUDY

The apostle John closes his Gospel with these words: "Jesus did many other miraculous signs in the presence of his disciples, which are not recorded in this book. But these are written that you may believe that Jesus is the Christ, the Son of God, and that by believing you may have life in his name" (John 20:30-31).

John writes about Jesus healing the blind and the sick on a number of occasions, such as this story in chapter 5. ***Read John 5:1-9.***

*[1]Some time later, Jesus went up to Jerusalem for a feast of the Jews. [2]Now there is in Jerusalem near the Sheep Gate a pool, which in Aramaic is called Bethesda and which is surrounded by five covered colonnades. [3]Here a great number of disabled people used to lie—the blind, the lame, the paralyzed.*** *[5]One who was there had been an invalid for thirty-eight years. [6]When Jesus saw him lying there and learned that he had been in this condition for a long time, he asked him, "Do you want to get well?"*

[7]"Sir," the invalid replied, "I have no one to help me into the pool when the water is stirred. While I am trying to get in, someone else goes down ahead of me."

[8]Then Jesus said to him, "Get up! Pick up your mat and walk." [9]At once the man was cured; he picked up his mat and walked.

**The end of verse 3 and verse 4, omitted here, are not included in most significant ancient manuscripts.

1. Picture the scene that Jesus saw as he went up to Jerusalem. Describe its setting and action.

2. How long does John tell us that one man had been there? Upon seeing the man, what is Jesus' initial response to him?

3. What surprises you about Jesus' question in verse 6?

Why do you think he asks this?

4. What do you make of the man's reply and Jesus' subsequent command?

Workers repairing a sewage pipe in the Old City of Jerusalem have discovered the biblical Pool of Siloam, a freshwater reservoir that was a major gathering place for ancient Jews making religious pilgrimages to the city and the reputed site where Jesus cured a man blind from birth, according to the Gospel of John.

"The pool was fed by the now famous Hezekiah's Tunnel and is 'a much grander affair' than archeologists previously believed, with three tiers of stone stairs allowing easy access to the water," said Hershel Shanks, editor of the *Biblical Archaeology Review,* which reported the find Monday.

"Scholars have said that there wasn't a Pool of Siloam and that John was using a religious conceit" to illustrate a point, said New Testament scholar James H. Charlesworth of the Princeton Theological Seminary.

"Now we have found the Pool of Siloam . . . exactly where

John said it was." A gospel that was thought to be "pure theology is now shown to be grounded in history," he said.

When ancient workmen were plastering the steps before facing them with stones, they either accidentally or deliberately buried four coins in the plaster. All four are coins of Alexander Jannaeus, a Jewish king who ruled Jerusalem from 103 to 76 B.C. That provides the earliest date at which the pool could have been constructed.

Similarly, in the soil in one corner of the pool, they found about a dozen coins dating from the period of the First Jewish Revolt against Rome, which lasted from A.D. 66 to 70. That indicates the pool had begun to be filled in by that time.

"Because the pool sits at one of the lowest spots in Jerusalem, rains flowing down the valley deposited mud into it each winter. It was no longer being cleaned out, so the pool quickly filled with dirt and disappeared," Shanks said.[2]

5. According to Hershel Shanks and James Charlesworth, what inaccurate assumptions were overturned upon this major archaeological find?

6. Although John—like other biblical writers—gives attention to literary effect, this discovery verifies that John was not taking poetic license ("using religious conceit"). "A gospel that was thought to be 'pure theology is now shown to be grounded in history.' " How might such a discovery change a person's preconceptions about the Gospel of John?

[2]Thomas H. Maugh II, "Biblical Pool Uncovered in Jerusalem," *The Los Angeles Times* (August 9, 2005).

In the Old Testament corroborating the presence of events is hard. Most events are singly attested, and the distance of time traversed since their occurrence is great. It is here that archaeological work helps us gain perspective. Often what was claimed to be known by more skeptical readers of the Old Testament at the turn into the twentieth century has been shown to be suspect by the work of archaeologists. The discovery of additional sites and artifacts from the ancient world fills large gaps in our knowledge.

The art of writing was said to be late, not pre-dating the time of David and certainly too late to allow Moses to be an author of the first five Old Testament books. In the first decade of the twentieth century, the Gezar Calendar was found. It dated from 925 B.C. and was written in Hebrew. Then a huge collection of Ugaritic texts was found in 1929. They date from 1400 B.C. and are in a language more closely related to Hebrew than any other ancient language. Earlier discoveries at Ras Shamra revealed Phoenician writing in the 1500 B.C. period. Pots with writing on them in Palestine were found in 1958 and 1960. So the idea that writing was not possible for the period became discredited. In fact, just recently proto-Sinaitic inscriptions have been found dating back to 1900 B.C., long before Moses.

7. What do the coins that were found in the Pool of Siloam reveal about the dating of Jesus' ministry and John's Gospel?

8. What does the recent discovery of ancient writing collections demonstrate regarding the authenticity and dating of some of the earliest Old Testament books?

9. How does archaeology assist us in studying and confirming events in the Old Testament?

10. Look again at the passage from John 5. Imagine being present when Jesus healed the man who had been an invalid for 38 years. Describe your response to this scene as if you were there.

11. Before Jesus heals the man, he asks him, "Do you want to get well?" In what ways would you like Jesus to help you? What would give you greater confidence in his ability to help?

■ GOING FURTHER

Take time to journal or discuss with someone your thoughts about this study, perhaps focusing on question 11. Might God be awaiting your response to him or his Word before you are able to move in a certain direction?

Additional Reading

Hershel Shanks, "Where Jesus Cured the Blind Man," *Biblical Archaeology Review* (September/October 2005), pp. 16-23 (available online at www.bib-arch.org/siloam.pdf).

6 Why Should We Obey the Bible?

JAMES 1:22-27

Scripture is far more than a history book, as good and trustworthy as that history is. It is a book that calls on us to examine our lives and relationship to God. Beyond the fascinating history, it contains vital and life-transforming truths about God and us. It is worth reading, studying and pondering for reasons that extend far beyond the history it so faithfully records.

■ OPEN

Think of a song, book or movie you know by heart. What drew you to it? What has made it so memorable for you?

■ STUDY

James, the brother of Jesus, writes his letter to fellow followers of Jesus living in a culture hostile to Christianity. He begins his book with a sermon of hope and perspective in the face of hardship and persecution. With pastoral empathy, he cautions his audience about the subtlety of self-deception and exhorts us to examine ourselves lest we forget who we are and who we were created to be. ***Read James 1:22-27.***

[22]*Do not merely listen to the word, and so deceive yourselves. Do what*

it says. [23]Anyone who listens to the word but does not do what it says is like a man who looks at his face in a mirror [24]and, after looking at himself, goes away and immediately forgets what he looks like. [25]But the man who looks intently into the perfect law that gives freedom, and continues to do this, not forgetting what he has heard, but doing it—he will be blessed in what he does.

[26]If anyone considers himself religious and yet does not keep a tight rein on his tongue, he deceives himself and his religion is worthless. [27]Religion that God our Father accepts as pure and faultless is this: to look after orphans and widows in their distress and to keep oneself from being polluted by the world.

1. James uses an *imperative* (a command) twice in verse 22. Why would a writer choose to use this form?

2. What simile does James employ? How does it illustrate his instruction in verse 22?

3. What memorable metaphor for the Scriptures do we find in verse 25?

What promises are given to those who give attention and obedience to the Word?

4. Verses 26 and 27 offer very practical—and yes, somewhat difficult—insight regarding what a child of God looks like. What are some ways people become polluted by the world today?

How might God help us guard against such pollution?

Judaism, and the Christianity that grew out of it, was a culture of memory, where the basic elements of an account were retained. People memorized long liturgical prayers and more often than not worked from memory rather than from a written page. Anyone who has read a children's book again and again to their child knows that the mind is capable of absorbing vast amounts of wording and retaining it. My daughters, when they were three, used to delight in finishing the sentences of their favorite stories. For ancient Jews, working orally was the norm, not the exception. It is perhaps hard for us to appreciate as modern people so used to the written word what it was like to habitually work with the oral word.

5. If you had limited access to the written word, what verses of Scripture would you want to memorize? Why?

The transformation that the message in the Bible brought to those who experienced the events is compelling testimony to its veracity. It was enough to cause people to leave everything and risk everything, including their lives, for what was taught. In sum, the Bible is historically trustworthy.

The case is strongest where it matters most—in its portrayal of Jesus. This is why we have concentrated on the New Testament and the Gospels. Strong historical support exists for a credible portrait of Jesus, despite loud claims otherwise often surfacing in the media. The biblical material points to a figure who challenged the religious leadership of Judaism and who made claims to be a uniquely sent representative of God. He brought to realization promises made long ago.

6. How does personal transformation provide "compelling testimony to [the Bible's] veracity"?

7. How does the thought that Jesus "brought to realization promises made long ago" contribute to your confidence in the reliability of the Scriptures?

8. In what ways has this study revealed more clearly who you are and are created to be?

9. Consider again James's analogy of the Scripture as a mirror. How have you changed during the course of this entire six-part study since examining yourself in this mirror? What further change would you like to see?

■ GOING FURTHER

Take time to journal or talk with someone further about your response to this study, giving thought to one particular feature of Scripture (such as inspiration or historicity) or a biblical passage examined.

Additional Reading

Eugene Peterson, *A Long Obedience in the Same Direction: Revised and Expanded Edition* (Downers Grove, Ill.: InterVarsity Press, 2000).

Leader's Notes

Leading a small group discussion can be an enjoyable and rewarding experience. But it can also be *scary*—especially if you've never done it before. If this is your feeling, you're in good company. When God asked Moses to lead the Israelites out of Egypt, he replied, "O LORD, please send someone else to do it" (Ex 4:13). It was the same with Solomon, Jeremiah and Timothy, but God helped these people in spite of their weaknesses, and he will help you as well.

You don't need to be an expert on the Bible or a trained teacher to lead a group discussion. The idea behind these studies is that the leader guides group members in their exploration of critical questions in the life of faith. This method of learning will allow group members to remember much more of what is said than a lecture would.

These studies are designed to be led easily. As a matter of fact, the flow of questions is so natural that you may feel that the studies lead themselves. This study guide is also flexible. You can use it with a variety of groups—student, professional, neighborhood or church groups. Each study takes around sixty minutes in a group setting.

There are some important facts to know about group dynamics

and encouraging discussion. The suggestions listed below should enable you to effectively and enjoyably fulfill your role as leader.

■ PREPARING FOR THE STUDY

1. Ask God to help you understand and apply the material in each session for your own life. Unless this happens, you will not be prepared to lead others. Pray too for the various members of the group. Ask God to open your hearts to the message of his Word and motivate you to action.

2. Read the introduction to the entire guide to get an overview of the entire book and the issues that will be explored.

3. As you begin each study, read and reread the assigned material to familiarize yourself with it.

4. Carefully work through each question in the study. Spend time in meditation and reflection as you consider how to respond.

5. Write your thoughts and responses in the space provided in the study guide. This will help you to express your understanding of the material clearly.

6. It might help to have a Bible dictionary handy. Use it to look up any unfamiliar words, names or places. (For additional help on how to study a passage, see chapter five of *How to Lead a LifeGuide Bible Study,* InterVarsity Press.)

7. Consider how the Scripture applies to your life. Remember that the group will follow your lead in responding to the studies. They will not go any deeper than you do.

8. Once you have finished your own study of the passage, familiarize yourself with the leader's notes for the study you are leading. These are designed to help you in several ways. First, they tell you the purpose the study guide author had in mind when writing the study. Take time to think through how the study questions work together to accomplish that purpose. Second, the notes provide you with additional background information for various questions. This information can be useful when people have difficulty understanding or answering a question. Third, the leader's notes can alert you to potential problems you may encounter during the study.

9. If you wish to remind yourself of anything mentioned in the leader's notes, make a note to yourself below that question in the study.

■ LEADING THE STUDY

1. Begin the study on time. Open with prayer, asking God to help the group to understand and apply the material being discussed.

2. Be sure that everyone in your group has a study guide. Encourage the group to prepare beforehand for each discussion by reading the introduction to the guide and by working through the questions in that week's session.

3. At the beginning of your first time together, explain that these studies are meant to be discussions, not lectures. Encourage the members of the group to participate. However, do not put pressure on those who may be hesitant to speak during the first few sessions. You may want to suggest the following guidelines to your group.

- Stick to the topic being discussed.
- Your responses should be based on the material provided and not on outside authorities such as commentaries or speakers.

- Only rarely should you refer to other portions of the Bible. This allows for everyone to participate in in-depth study on equal ground.
- Anything said in the group is considered confidential and will not be discussed outside the group unless specific permission is given to do so.
- We will listen attentively to each other and provide time for each person present to talk.
- We will pray for each other.

4. Have a group member read the introduction at the beginning of the discussion.

5. Every session begins with a group discussion question. The question or activity is meant to be used before the passage is read. The question introduces the theme of the study and encourages group members to begin to open up. Encourage as many members as possible to participate, and be ready to get the discussion going with your own response.

This section is designed to reveal where our thoughts or feelings need to be transformed by the renewing of our minds. That is why it is especially important not to read the passage to the group members before the discussion question is asked. The passage will tend to color the honest reactions people would otherwise give because they are, of course, supposed to think the way the Bible does.

You may want to supplement the group discussion question with an icebreaker to help people to get comfortable. See the community section of *Small Group Idea Book* for more ideas.

6. Have a group member (or members if the passage is long) read aloud the textual material as it occurs in the session. Then give people several minutes to read the passage again silently so that they can take it all in.

7. As you ask the questions, keep in mind that they are designed to be used just as they are written. You may simply read them aloud. Or you may prefer to express them in your own words. There may be times when it is appropriate to deviate from the study guide. For example, a question may have already been answered. If so, move on to the next question. Or someone may raise an important question not covered in the guide. Take time to discuss it, but try to keep the group from going off on tangents.

8. Avoid answering your own questions. If necessary, repeat or rephrase them until they are clearly understood. Or point out something you read in the leader's notes to clarify the context or meaning. An eager group quickly becomes passive and silent if they think the leader will do most of the talking.

9. Don't be afraid of silence. People may need time to think about the question before formulating their answers.

10. Don't be content with just one answer. Ask, "What do the rest of you think?" or "Anything else?" until several people have given answers to the question.

11. Acknowledge all contributions. Try to be affirming whenever possible. Never reject an answer. If it is clearly off-base, ask, "Which verse led you to that conclusion?" or again, "What do the rest of you think?"

12. Don't expect every answer to be addressed to you, even though this will probably happen at first. As group members become more at ease, they will begin to truly interact with each other. This is one sign of healthy discussion.

13. Don't be afraid of controversy. It can be very stimulating. If you don't resolve an issue completely, don't be frustrated. Move on and keep it in mind for later. A subsequent study may solve the problem.

14. Periodically summarize what the group has said to that point. This helps to draw together the various ideas mentioned and gives continuity to the discussion. But don't preach.

15. Give an opportunity during the session for people to talk about what they are learning.

16. Conclude your time together with conversational prayer. Ask for God's help in working through the implications of the discussion.

17. End on time.

■ COMPONENTS OF SMALL GROUPS

A healthy small group should do more than study the Bible. There are four components to consider as you structure your time together.

- *Nurture.* Small groups help us to grow in our knowledge and love of God. Bible study is the key to making this happen and is the foundation of your small group.
- *Community.* Small groups are a great place to develop deep friendships with other Christians. Allow time for informal interaction before and after each discussion. Plan activities and games that will help you get to know each other. Spend time having fun together—going on a picnic or cooking dinner together.
- *Worship and prayer.* Your study will be enhanced by spending time

praising God together in prayer or song. Pray for each other's needs—and keep track of how God is answering prayer in your group. Ask God to help you to apply what you are learning in your study.

- *Outreach.* Reaching out to others can be a practical way of applying what you are learning, and it will keep your group from becoming self-focused. Host a series of evangelistic discussions for your friends or neighbors. Clean up the yard of an elderly friend. Serve at a soup kitchen together, or spend a day working on a Habitat house.

Many more suggestions and helps in each of these areas are found in *Small Group Idea Book.* Information on building a small group can be found in *Small Group Leaders' Handbook* and *The Big Book on Small Groups* (both from InterVarsity Press). Reading through one of these books would be worth your time.

STUDY 1

How Did We Get the Bible We Have?

MATTHEW 5:17-20

***Purpose:* To show that Jesus affirmed the authority and trustworthiness of the Scriptures.**

QUESTION 1. "The Law and the Prophets" is a common expression referring to the canon of the Old Testament. See, for example, Matthew 11:13; Acts 24:14; 28:23; Romans 3:21. For further statements from Jesus on the Law and the Prophets, see Matthew 7:12 and 22:40.

QUESTION 2. Compare what Jesus says in verse 17 about "fulfill" with his remarks in Matthew 26:53-54. Many scholars have noted, as

R. T. France writes, "The essential key to all of Matthew's theology is that in Jesus all God's purposes have come to fulfillment. This is, of course, true of all New Testament theology, but it is emphasized in a remarkable way in Matthew. Everything is related to Jesus. . . . Matthew leaves no room for any idea of the fulfillment of God's purposes, whether for Israel or in any other respect, which is not focused in this theme of *fulfillment in Jesus*. In his coming a new age has dawned; nothing will ever be quite the same again" (R. T. France, *Matthew,* Tyndale New Testament Commentaries [Downers Grove, Ill.: InterVarsity Press, 1992], p. 38).

QUESTION 3. Earlier in Matthew 5, Jesus speaks tenderly toward his disciples; compare Matthew 5:1-16 to his direct words about the Scriptures and himself in verses 17-20.

QUESTIONS 4-5. Discussion has existed about the inclusion/exclusion of some Old Testament books known today as the Apocrypha or the Deutero-canonicals. However, the thirty-nine books of the Old Testament, excluding the Apocrypha, have been recognized as canonical in Judaism almost since the time of Christ. The first century Jewish historian Josephus tells us that there are not "an innumerable multitude of books among us, disagreeing and contradicting one another [as the Greeks have], but only twenty-two books, which contain the records of past times" (*Against Apion* 1.38). He then names the five books of Moses, thirteen prophets and four books of hymns and precepts alluding to, among others, Psalms and Proverbs. Josephus' twenty-two books follow the Jewish divisions of the Old Testament: Torah, Prophets (including the historical books and including the twelve prophets as a group) and Writings. Qumran texts also attest to this basic division with the expression "the book of Moses, the words of the prophets and of David."

QUESTION 6. As Ravi Zacharias has written, we cannot escape the fact that each of us esteems some books or ideas as canonical (authoritative) and others as not. Therefore, the question is, *What evidence leads us to our conclusions, and is the evidence trustworthy?* "I have heard questions that are deep and complex sometimes coming even from young teenagers, but the solutions I have heard most often offered to them are, quite frankly, superficial and simple. Many frustrated young people have expressed, 'All I hear my parents or preachers saying is that the Bible says this is so and therefore, it is so, and that is the only answer necessary to give. What they do not realize,' the young person passionately pleads, 'is that when I begin my answer at school (or in the university) with 'the Bible says,' my answer is immediately dismissed as irrelevant, and in some instances I am torn to bits.' I often remind them that the same type of 'authority referencing' is given by the irreligious person who also provides no defense for why their source has served as canonical for them, be it this philosopher or that movie-star. Both starting points undefended are open to question" (Ravi Zacharias, *Can Man Live Without God?* [Dallas: Word, 1994], p. 13).

QUESTION 7. There is no doubt that some of the catalyst for identifying the New Testament canon was motivated by disputes that broke out concerning Christian teaching in the early centuries after the birth of the new faith. The dispute with Marcion around A.D. 140 seems to have really given impetus to this effort to identify the received books. (Marcion rejected the Old Testament because he had difficulty reconciling the God of the Old Testament with the God of the New Testament.) After all, some Christian subgroups and fringe groups wrote their own documents, claiming to possess authority for all the church. In addition, the reading of sacred texts as a part of worship required that those books be identified. A process of sorting out the valuable from the spurious began, and the church proceeded carefully and took a few centuries to settle on the matter. What is crucial to appreciate here is that the church did not pick the books of the canon but undertook a process to recognize them. They received only those books they regarded as giving evidence of divine authority.

QUESTION 8. Many people, skeptics and believers alike, have wrestled with whether the Bible is really God's Word. Yet Ravi Zacharias often observes that it is critical to understand that when someone raises a difficult academic question, you must always consider that there may be a greater existential concern behind their intellectual question. In other words, does the individual's question about the reliability of the Scriptures actually cover over the deeper uncertainty or even anger that one may be feeling about God's own trustworthiness and care for them? Hence, the second part of question 8: "*When* does this question seem to surface for you?" For further reading, see Ravi Zacharias's *Cries of the Heart: Bringing God Near When He Feels So Far Away* (Nashville: Word, 1998), especially chapter one, "The Cry to Know God" (pp. 1-30).

QUESTION 9. Though the NIV uses the word "break," commentators show that "relax" (RSV) or "set aside" is a better understanding of what Jesus is communicating. That is, those who dismiss or relax the Scriptures' authority and teaching disregard Jesus' own assertions of its authority—and indeed invalidate ("annul") it. R. T. France writes, "Like the previous two verses, this one warns the disciples against altering or setting aside any part of the law, however small. (*Relaxes* is from the same root as *abolish* in v. 17, and means to 'set aside' or 'teach against' a commandment, rather than to disobey it.) . . . That this is Jesus' teaching for his own disciples, not a traditional Jewish saying, is indicated *by the kingdom of heaven:* disrespect for the Old Testament makes a poor Christian. . . . The good disciple will *do* and *teach* the commandments: he will go beyond lip-service, to be guided by them in his life and teaching" (France, *Matthew,* pp. 115-16).

QUESTION 10. "This verse dispels any suspicion of legalism which v. 19 might have raised. The *scribes* (professional students and teachers of the law) *and Pharisees* (members of a largely lay movement devoted to scrupulous observance both of the Old Testament law and of the still developing legal traditions), whose obedience to 'the least of these commandments' could not be faulted, do not thereby qualify for *the kingdom of heaven* (whereas the disciple who relaxes the commandments does belong to it, though as the 'least'). What is required is a greater *righteousness* (see on 3:15; 5:6,10), a relationship of love and obedience to God which is more than a literal observance of regulations. It is such a 'righteousness' which fulfills the law and the prophets (v. 17), and which will be illustrated in vv. 21-48 (in contrast with the legalism of the scribes)" (France, *Matthew,* p. 116).

QUESTION 11. In Matthew 6:31-33 Jesus describes his heavenly Father's tender care for his disciples and what this trusting relationship looks like: "So do not worry, saying, 'What shall we eat?' or 'What shall we drink?' or 'What shall we wear?' For the pagans run after all these things, and *your heavenly Father knows that you need them.* But seek first his kingdom and his righteousness, and all these things will be given to you as well." Commenting on Matthew 3:15, R. T. France writes, "*Righteousness* in Matthew is not so much 'being good', still less legal correctness, but rather a synonym for the Christian life, viewed as a *relationship* [emphasis mine] with God focused in obedience" (p. 94).

STUDY 2

What Are Our Sources?

LUKE 1:1-4; 3:1-6

***Purpose:* To establish that the biblical authors' precision reveals they are a reliable source of information about God and our world.**

OPEN. Have the group experiment with the telephone game. Have one member whisper the opening paragraph from the study to the person on his or her right, who then repeats it verbally (without looking at the study) to the next person, and so on. The last person then writes down what's whispered and reads it out loud to the group.

QUESTION 1. "Luke's preface fits the ancient pattern in which a writer explains the rationale for his work (2 Maccabees 2:19-31; Josephus *Antiquities* . . . and Lucian *How to Write History* . . .). Luke consciously introduces his work to show where it fits in ancient literary terms. Some speak of Luke as 'apologetic historiography' . . . but Luke is writing more for internal exhortation, so that any apologetic has a pastoral purpose" (Darrell Bock, *Luke,* The IVP New Testament Commentary Series [Downers Grove, Ill.: InterVarsity Press, 1994], pp. 30-31).

QUESTION 2. "Four characteristics mark Luke's approach to his task. First, he *investigated* ***(parēkolouthēkoti)*** the story. This appears to refer to the fact that he studied the topic. . . . Second, Luke went back to *the beginning* ***(anōthen)***. This is why the story starts with John the Baptist. . . . Third, his study was thorough: he says he studied *everything* ***(pasin)***. Though what we have in Luke is surely a select collection of material, the Gospel writer wants it known that he did his homework. Luke was very concerned to get his story right, to be accurate in his portrayal of Jesus. Fourth, Luke did his work *carefully* *(akribōs)* . . . and calls his account an *orderly* one *(kathexēs)*" (Bock, *Luke*, pp. 32-33).

QUESTION 3. "Both volumes are addressed to Theophilus (Lk 1:1-4; Acts 1:1-4). We know nothing else about this individual. To determine Theophilus's concerns we must look carefully at the text. We do know he needed reassurance. The amount of material about preserving in the Christian life suggests that he is already a Christian rather than a person coming to Christ. In fact, the whole emphasis on Gentile inclusion, which continues through Acts, suggests that Theophilus is a Gentile who finds himself in an originally Jewish movement" (Bock, *Luke*, p. 18).

QUESTION 4. Regarding biblical sources, occasionally such sources are named (2 Kings 15:26, 31). In other cases, we do not know what the exact sources of information were. This makes exact corroboration hard to establish, but that is a fact for *virtually all* the events we work with from ancient history, many of which we accept without *any* parallel accounts.

We do know that within Judaism there existed the ability to pass things on with care from one generation to the next. This does not mean that one necessarily passed on the contents word for word, but it does mean that the recounting of events was done with care for the core of the story. That some variation took place in telling an event is obvious by comparing the Gospels' accounts or Samuel-Kings-Chronicles to one another. One can see the same trend in comparing rabbinical parallel accounts to one another. What we also see in general is *a recognizable core* to the account.

QUESTION 5. "Luke's stress here is the credibility of the sources, since they saw firsthand what has been described in the tradition. Luke makes a key point—the tradition about Jesus had roots in the experience of those who preached about him. These witnesses were with Jesus from the beginning. Thus these first two verses mention at least two generations: those who preached Jesus and those who recorded what was preached. There was precedent for what Luke was doing, both in terms of larger ancient history and in terms of the story of Jesus" (Bock, *Luke*, pp. 31-32).

QUESTION 6. Luke's citing of specific persons allow us to date John the Baptist's ministry between A.D. 27 and 29. Biblical scholar Leon Morris comments, "Luke adds a dating of peculiar importance to Jews, namely with reference to *the high-priesthood. Annas* was high priest A.D. 6-15, when the Roman governor Gratus deposed him. Five of his sons became high priest in due course, and *Caiaphas,* who held the office A.D. 18-36, was his son-in-law. Luke uses the singular, which shows that he knew there was only one high priest. He appears to mean that Caiaphas was actually in office, but that Annas still exercised great influence, perhaps even was regarded by the Jews as the true high priest (*cf.* Acts 4:6). . . . It may be worth pointing out that when Jesus was arrested he was first brought to Annas (Jn. 18:13)" (Leon Morris, *Luke,* Tyndale New Testament Commentaries [Downers Grove, Ill.: InterVarsity Press, 1994], p. 104).

QUESTION 7. It is significant to note that Luke uses the verb "to repent" and noun "repentance" more often than Matthew, Mark and John put together (Morris, *Luke,* p. 104). "John called on people to turn away from their sins and the acceptance of his baptism was a sign that they had done this," adds Morris. "The purpose was *forgiveness*. Baptism was a rite of cleansing in a number of religions. It seems certain that at this time the Jews used proselyte baptism, a ceremony to cleanse converts from the defilement they saw as characteristic of all Gentiles. The sting in John's practice was that he applied to Jews the ceremony they regarded as suitable for unclean Gentiles. John denounces those who expected that in the judgment God would deal hardly with Gentile sinners, but that the Jews, the descendants of Abraham, would be safe. He removes this fancied security" (*Luke*, pp. 104-5).

QUESTION 8. Luke's quoting of Isaiah 40:3-5 is significant, for he envisions John the Baptist's ministry as a direct fulfillment of Isaiah's prophecy concerning the coming of the Lord. John is a forerunner to Jesus (see also Gabriel's pronouncement in Luke 1:16-17) and one who, like Elijah, would prepare hearts for the way of the Lord. "The passage itself compares preparing for the events of salvation to preparing a red-carpet reception for a king. The creation is called to level the path so God can enter. With his entry God makes salvation manifest for all to see. There is nowhere else to look for God's saving work except to Jesus. The appeal to the leveling of creation is best seen as including the removing of moral obstacles to God's arrival. John is the sentry who issues the moral call to clear the way for his coming" (Bock, *Luke*, p. 67).

QUESTION 9. Amy Orr-Ewing, training director for Ravi Zacharias International Ministries in the U.K., writes, "Before the discovery of the scrolls, the oldest known manuscript was 1,300 years after the writing of the complete Old Testament. After the finding of the scrolls, the problem was then to ascertain how accurate these manuscripts were in relation to what was originally written. Because the text had been copied many times, could it be trusted? One of the scrolls had a complete copy of Isaiah in Hebrew. It is dated by paleographers around 125 B.C.; with the Masoretic text being A.D. 916, this makes a difference of 1,000 years. If, upon examination, there were little or no textual changes in those Masoretic texts where comparisons were possible, an assumption could then be made that the Masoretic Scribes had probably been just as faithful in their copying of the other biblical texts which could not be compared with the Qumran material.

"The accuracy is astonishing for an ancient manuscript and is word for word identical with our standard Hebrew Bible in 95 percent of the text. In the other 5 percent there are only minor variations. To give an example, of the 166 words in Isaiah 53 there are 17 letters in question:

- Ten of these are a matter of spelling which does not affect the sense.
- Four are minor stylistic changes, such as conjunctions.
- The remaining 3 letters comprise the word 'light' which is added in verse 11 and does not affect the meaning greatly. In fact the use of 'light' here is supported by two other manuscripts, the LXX ('Septuagint', the Greek translation of the Old Testament) and the IQ Isa ('Isaiah A', a copy of Isaiah found in Cave 1 at Qumran).

(Amy Orr-Ewing, *Is the Bible Intolerant?* [Downers Grove, Ill.: InterVarsity Press, 2006], p. 46).

STUDY 3

What Do We Mean by *Inspiration?*

2 PETER 1:16-21

***Purpose:* To show that the Scriptures declare that God is the origin and inspiration of the words of the biblical writers.**

QUESTION 1. John 1:35-42 describes Jesus' first encounter with Peter and his brother Andrew. Mark 1:16-18 and 3:13-16 record Jesus' calling and subsequent appointment of Peter as one of his twelve disciples. The Gospel writers go on to portray Peter as one who was intimately acquainted with Jesus.

QUESTION 2. Peter is referring here to the transfiguration of Jesus, which he witnessed with James and John. Matthew, Mark and Luke each record this event. See Matthew 16:28—17:8; Mark 9:2-8; Luke 9:28-36.

QUESTION 3. Peter expresses his awe with a very rare word, ***megaleiotēs*** ("majesty"), which occurs only two other times in the New Testament (see Lk 9:43; Acts 19:27). All three occurrences refer to the majesty of the Divine (Michael Green, *2 Peter & Jude,* Tyndale New Testament Commentaries [Downers Grove, Ill.: InterVarsity Press, 1987], p. 93).

QUESTION 5. Pastor and scholar Michael Green comments, "It is interesting that in this, perhaps the fullest and most explicit biblical reference to the inspiration of its authors, no interest should be displayed in the psychology of inspiration. The author is not concerned with what they felt like, or how much they understood, but simply with the fact that they were bearers of God's message. The relative parts played by the human and divine authors are not mentioned, but only the fact of their co-operation. He uses a fascinating maritime metaphor in verse 21 (*cf.* Acts 27:15, 17, where the same word, ***pheromenē,*** is used of a ship carried along by the wind). The prophets raised their sails, so to speak (they were obedient and receptive), and the Holy Spirit filled them and carried their craft along in the direction he wished. Men spoke: God spoke. Any proper doctrine of Scripture will not neglect either part of this truth" (Green, *2 Peter & Jude*, pp. 102-3).

QUESTION 6. "From personal eyewitness testimony Peter now turns to 'the prophetic word.' As in all other occurrences of the term, Peter means the Old Testament, and he adduces it in support for his teachings in verses 3-11. The crucial word is ***bebaioteron****, more certain.* Does it mean that the Scriptures confirm the apostolic witness (AV, NEB [margin])? Or does it mean that the apostolic witness fulfils, and thus authenticates, Scripture (RV, RSV, NEB, NIV)? . . .

"The Jews always preferred prophecy to the voice from heaven. Indeed, they regarded the latter, the ***bath qōl***, 'daughter of the voice', as an inferior substitute for revelation, since the days of prophecy had ceased. And as for the apostles, it is hard to overemphasize their regard for the Old Testament. One of the most powerful arguments for the truth of Christianity was the argument from prophecy (see the speeches in Acts, Rom. 15; 1 Pet. 2, or the whole of Heb. or Rev.). In the word of God written, they sought absolute assurance, like their Master, for whom 'it is written' sufficed to clinch an argument. Peter's meaning seems to be that given in the first alternative above. He is saying, 'If you don't believe me, go to the Scriptures'. 'The question', says Calvin, is not whether the prophets are more trustworthy than the gospel.' It is simply that 'since the Jews were in no doubt that everything that the prophets taught came from God, it is no wonder that Peter says that their word is more sure'" (Green, *2 Peter & Jude,* pp. 97-98).

QUESTION 8. For further insight, see 2 Peter 2:1-3. Notice also the comparative words "Above all" in verse 20, which emphasize Peter's argument in the preceding section. The apostle not only rejects "cleverly invented stories" (v. 16) and "the prophet's own interpretation" (v. 20) but also contrasts these two illegitimate sources of information with prophecy inspired by the Holy Spirit.

QUESTIONS 9-10. Michael Green contends, "The same God whom the apostles heard speak in the transfiguration spoke also through the prophets. The argument in verses 20-21 is a consistent and indeed necessary conclusion to the preceding paragraph. Thus, we can rely on the apostolic account of the transfiguration because God spoke. And we can rely on Scripture because behind its human authors God spoke. The prophets did not make up what they wrote. They did not arbitrarily unravel it. 'They did not blab their inventions of their own accord or according to their own judgments' (Calvin). In the Old Testament, this was the characteristic of the false prophets, who 'speak visions from their own minds, not from the mouth of the Lord' (Je. 23:16, *cf.* Ezk. 13:3). But true prophecy came from God and, men as they were, the prophets were *carried along* by the Holy Spirit.

"Peter, then, is talking about the divine origin of the Scriptures, not about its proper interpretation. . . .

"It should now be apparent that Peter has been replying to two charges by false teachers. To their contention that the apostles were purveying myths about Jesus, his power and coming, Peter says 'Not so: we were with him at the transfiguration. We were eyewitnesses.' He then adduces the Old Testament as a witness which is even more unimpeachable than the apostles themselves. . . . But they respond by rejecting the authority of the Old Testament, denying its divine origin, and saying that the prophets simply produced their own ideas. So Peter strongly reasserts the conviction, common to Jews, Jesus and Christians alike, that the Old Testament has indeed a divine origin, and when the prophets spoke about the prophecies recorded in Scripture they were men in touch with God who acted as spokesmen" (Green, *2 Peter & Jude,* pp. 101-2).

STUDY 4

What Is the History Behind the Bible?

MATTHEW 21:18-22; MARK 11:12-25

Purpose: **To show that the biblical writers recorded historical events with attention to both accuracy and literary effect.**

OPEN. Though each individual is unique, scholars have observed a difference between the ways men and women commonly retell an experience or a story. That is, more often men compress details and offer skeletal factual information whereas women tend to explore emotions and look for a connection with their listener.

QUESTION 1. Interestingly, Mark tells us that Jesus cursed the fig tree though he knew that "it was not the season for figs" (v. 13). The only point one need make regarding this verse is that Mark offers insight into Jesus' actions that Matthew does not. However, should questions arise, Mark's parenthetical explanation is an allusion to what he will develop further in this passage as he explores Jesus' actions: in cursing the tree out of season, Jesus demonstrates his God-given sovereignty and judgment over nature and our world. The late Mark Lane commented: "*Events have meaning beyond their face value; they become significant as they are interpreted.* The unexpected and incongruous character of Jesus' action in looking for figs at a season when no fruit could be found would stimulate curiosity and point beyond the incident to its deeper significance. His act was an example of prophetic realism [that is, a zeal for God's laws and nations] similar to the symbolic actions of the OT prophets (e.g. Isa. 20:1-6; Jer. 13:1-11; 19:1-13; Ezek. 4:1-15)" (Mark Lane, *The Gospel According to Mark: The English Text with Introduction, Exposition, and Notes,* New International Commentary on the New Testament [Grand Rapids: Eerdmans, 1974], p. 400, emphasis added).

QUESTION 2. R. T. France notes, "Careful communicator as he is, Matthew frequently omits incidental details which he regards as inessential to his purpose. Thus stories which in Mark are told in a lively, expansive style, with plenty of picturesque detail, regularly appear in Matthew in a much more concise form, boiled down to the bare essentials which are needed to convey the message Matthew wishes to draw out of the story. (*E.g.*, the stories which make up the 43 verses of Mark 5 take up only 16 verses in Matthew 8:28-34; 9:18-26.) The effect is that Matthew is less immediately attractive as a story-teller, but that the cumulative impression of his more taut narratives is very powerful in its portrayal of the overwhelming authority of Jesus" (R. T. France, *Matthew,* Tyndale New Testament Commentaries [Downers Grove, Ill.: InterVarsity Press, 1992], p. 22).

QUESTIONS 3-4. Whereas Matthew places Jesus' cleansing of the temple after his cursing of the fig tree, Mark divides the fig tree episode, framing the temple cleansing with Jesus' cursing the tree (vv. 12-14) and the curse's effect upon it (vv. 20-21). By dividing this story into three sections that each reveal God's judgment acted out, Mark further develops his theme (also prominent in the Old Testament's prophetic writings). Mark Lane observes: "The prophets frequently spoke of the fig tree in referring to Israel's status before God (e.g. Jer. 8:13, 29:17; Hos. 9:10, 16; Joel 1:7; Micah 7:1-6), while the destruction of the fig tree is associated with judgment (Hos. 2:12; Isa. 34:4; cf. Lk. 13:6-9). . . . In the Gospel of Mark Jesus' action in the Temple is firmly embedded within the fig tree incident. The a-b-a structure [fig tree-temple cleansing-fig tree] serves to provide a mutual commentary on these two events. Just as the leaves of the tree concealed the fact that there was no fruit to enjoy, so the magnificence of the Temple and its ceremony conceals the fact that Israel has not brought forth the fruit of righteousness demanded by God. Both incidents have the character of a prophetic sign which warns of judgment to fall upon Israel for honoring God with their lips when their heart was far from him (cf. [Mark] 7:6)" (Lane, *Gospel According to Mark,* p. 400).

QUESTIONS 6-7. To use these standards is not to say they are perfect or foolproof, but they are a way to get into a discussion about how one can show trustworthiness. Many events about Jesus are defendable as trustworthy at this level. A collection of events made at this level gives us enough to work with that we can make firm statements about Jesus' message and self understanding. The results are far more positive than anything the Jesus Seminar has argued.

The reality is we work with partial knowledge concerning the events we investigate. Our sources are limited. Sources speak partially, even when they are accurate. They also speak from a perspective, as we noted in the previous section, making them inherently limited in their point of view. This is so even when they are right about the facts they relate. Sources also only cover a portion what actually took place. They are selective. Even the Bible makes this point. In John 21:25 we read, "But there are many other things Jesus did; if every one of them were written done, I suppose that the world itself could not contain the books that would be written." If we knew these other things, we would know more about the subject. We would be able to say more about those events and assess more about them. When people give respect to the testimony of Scripture and call it trustworthy, they are arguing that its testimony is sufficient to give us a meaningful understanding of God and his work. They are not arguing that it tells us everything.

STUDY 5

What Does Archaeology Teach Us?

JOHN 5:1-15

***Purpose:* To show that archaeology supports the history and authenticity of the Scriptures.**

QUESTION 1. "To tell the story of the Pool of Siloam, where Jesus cured the blind man [see Jn 9], we must go back 700 years before that—to the time of the Assyrian monarch Sennacherib and his siege of Jerusalem. . . .

"The only source of fresh water at this time was the Gihon Spring, near the floor of the adjacent Kidron Valley. So Hezekiah decided on a major engineering project—he would construct a tunnel under the ridge on which the City of David lay to bring the water of the spring to the other, less vulnerable, side of Jerusalem. . . .

"The waters of Siloam are mentioned by the prophet Isaiah, a contemporary of Hezekiah's, who refers to 'the gently flowing waters of Siloam' (Shiloah in Hebrew) (Isaiah 8:6). When the exiles returned from Babylon and rebuilt the walls of Jerusalem, Nehemiah tells us that a certain Shallun rebuilt 'the wall of the Pool of Shiloah by the King's Garden' (Nehemiah 3:15). . . .

"In the Byzantine period the empress Eudocia (c. 400-460) built a church and a pool where the water debouches [emerges] from Hezekiah's Tunnel to commemorate the miracle of the blind man. Early in the last century archaeologists found the remains of that church, over which today sits a mosque. The church and the pool are mentioned in several Byzantine pilgrim itineraries. Until last year, it was this pool that people meant when they talked of the Pool of Siloam.

"Now we have found an earlier pool, the pool as it existed in Jesus' time—and it is a much grander affair" (Hershel Shanks, "Where Jesus

Cured the Blind Man," *Biblical Archaeology Review* [September/October 2005], pp. 16, 18).

QUESTION 2. The omitted ending of verse 3 and verse 4 read: "And they waited for the moving of the waters. [4]From time to time an angel of the Lord would come down and stir up the waters. The first one into the pool after each such disturbance would be cured of whatever disease he had." However, this text does not appear in the more important manuscripts, nor does it fit with a biblical understanding of the wideness of God's healing and mercy. We are led to wonder what more may be going on that John doesn't tell us. Did the man want to get well, or had he perhaps resigned his hope?

QUESTION 3. Rodney Whitacre offers this comment: "Although Jesus knows the man has been ill for a long time and also knows what is in his heart (2:24-25), he nevertheless initiates the contact by asking if he wants to get well (5:6). This Gospel stresses both divine sovereignty and human responsibility, and here we see both Jesus' sovereign approach to this man and the importance of the man's own will" (Rodney A. Whitacre, *John,* The IVP New Testament Commentary Series [Downers Grove, Ill.: InterVarsity Press, 1999], p. 119).

QUESTION 4. "What would we say to Jesus if he asked us whether we wanted to be healed of our own illnesses, physical or otherwise? Do we want to be rid of our addictions and other sins? Ten minutes hard thought on this question could lead us to new depths of repentance. It seems like a silly question—of course he would want to be healed. But perhaps this man has grown accustomed to his disability and would prefer known pain to the terror of the unknown, with its new responsibilities. While such speculation is true to human nature, John does not develop this line of thought. . . . He is, however, quite clear on the basic point that what one wants or wills or desires (all of these can be conveyed by the verb ***thēlo***) plays a vital role in determining whether one can recognize Christ and receive him (7:17). God finds each of us as helpless as this man. The good news is that he desires to grant each of us life, not necessarily mere healing in this life, but eternal life beginning now" (Whitacre, *John*, pp. 119-20).

QUESTION 10. Ravi Zacharias makes a crucial point in a similar discussion about the healing of a paralytic: " 'Which of the two is harder,' asked the Lord, 'to bring physical healing or to forgive a person's sins?' The irresistible answer was self-evident, was it not? To bring physical healing because that would be such a miraculous thing, visible to the naked eye. The invisible act of forgiveness had far less evidentiary value. Yet, as they pondered and as we ponder, we discover repeatedly in life that the logic of God is so different to the logic of humanity. We move from the material to the spiritual in terms of the spectacular, but God moves from the spiritual to the material in terms of the essential. The physical is the concrete external—a shadow. The spiritual is the intangible internal—the objective actuality. . . .

"In this instance, Jesus followed the act of forgiveness with the easier act of physical healing so that the paralyzed man would feel the touch of the Savior from what was more meaningful to what was more felt. If he was a wise man he would walk with the awareness that the apparently less visible miracle was actually more miraculous than the more visible one—but his feeling of gratitude for his restored body would remain a constant reminder to him of the restoration of his soul" (Ravi Zacharias, "Apologetics: Shadow or Reality?" *Just Thinking,* fall 2004, available online at www.rzim.org/publications/jttran.php?seqid=98).

QUESTION 11. Jesus asks such direct questions not to push away his petitioners but to invite them to put their profound longing into words. His pointed response to the man in John 5—"Do you want to get well?"—was not only an invitation to him; it is also a summons to us. Throughout the Gospels Jesus' presence and his insistent questions cast light on our unspoken desires, hesitations and fears, whether with the woman at the well (Jn 4) or the man at the Pool of Siloam. Notice that Jesus takes the initiative with both; he approaches them and inquires of their need.

STUDY 6

Why Should We Obey the Bible?

JAMES 1:22-27

Purpose: **To show that beyond its historicity, Scripture also calls us to respond to its author and content.**

QUESTION 1. Just as parents instruct and caution their children, James exhorts his readers "*Do not* merely listen to the word" but rather "*do* what it says." Moreover, just as attentive parents not only tell their children not to do something but also offer constructive counsel, James provides both negative and positive instruction to amplify his point.

QUESTION 2. Pastor and author George Stulac suggests, "James's analogy places emphasis on the usefulness of God's word for our salvation in daily living. . . . For the analogy of the mirror to be appropriate, James must have believed in both the perspicuity [clarity] and the applicability of Scripture. He believed the word of God to be clear and understandable, comparable to a mirror that gives an accurate reflection rather than one so clouded or distorted that the viewer would gain no real understanding from looking at it. James believed also that the word of God reveals matters upon which the readers should take some appropriate action; the word is relevant in application to our lives. People who are hearers only are deceiving themselves because they ignore these two features of the word of God. They treat the word as if it were useless because of being either unclear or irrelevant" (George M. Stulac, *James,* The IVP New Testament Commentary Series [Downers Grove, Ill.: InterVarsity Press, 1993], pp. 75-76).

QUESTION 3. The preceding passage says, "Humbly accept the word planted in you, which can save you" (v. 21). As a Jew, James was not only intimately familiar with the Old Testament but had also likely memorized much of it. As such, when James wrote of "the perfect law that gives freedom" he may have had in mind Psalm 19:7: "The law of the Lord is perfect, reviving the soul."

QUESTIONS 8-9. Ravi Zacharias views the disciples' transformation and the reliability of the Scriptures through the unique lens of Jesus' resurrection. In *Can Man Live Without God?* he writes, "When an honest reader looks at the affirmations that are made and the substantiations that are provided [in the New Testament], the following deductions ensue:

1. Jesus Christ Himself talked of His resurrection on repeated occasions. Both His enemies and His followers were told to expect it. Those who sought to smother His teaching took elaborate steps to counter the possibility of His claim, including the placement of a Roman guard at the door to the tomb.
2. Although His supporters basically understood His promise to rise from the dead and had even witnessed His raising of Lazarus,

they did not really believe that He meant it literally until after the fact. Therefore, they could not be accused of creating the scenario for this deception.

3. It was the post-resurrection appearance that made the ultimate difference to the skeptical mind of Thomas and the resistant will of Paul.

4. The transformation of the disciples from a terrified bunch of individuals who felt themselves betrayed into a fearless group ready to proclaim the message to Rome and to the rest of the world cannot be explained with a mere shrug of the shoulder.

5. Had the Roman authorities wanted to eradicate Jesus' teaching once and for all, they would have only needed to present His dead body—but they could not. . . .

6. One other very interesting factor to bring to our attention is from non-Christian sources. Even the Koran, which is hardly in favor of the Christian message, attests to Jesus' virgin birth and credits Him with the unique power to raise the dead, a most interesting notation often forgotten by the Muslims themselves.

"In summary, it was Jesus' victory over the grave that provided the grand impetus for the early church to tell the world that God had spoken and, indeed, had done so in a dramatic and incontrovertible manner. All this transpired in history and is open to the historian's scrutiny" (Ravi Zacharias, *Can Man Live Without God?* [Dallas: Word, 1994], pp. 162-63).